Servir

Copyrig

Contact address:

P O Bo:

Kanye

Botswana

E-mail address: otengmontshiti@gmail.com

Contact number: (+267) 74 644 954

Contents

Acknowledgements

Writing a book is a challenging task which requires time. I would like thank my family especially my lovely wife for supporting me.

Serving God
Introduction

Luke 4:18 The Spirit of the Lord *is* upon me, because he hath anointed me to preach the gospel to the poor; he hath sent me to heal the brokenhearted, to preach deliverance to the captives, and recovering of sight to the blind, to set at liberty them that are bruised,

Today, if proper care isn't taken infighting within the church of God is going to reach unprecedented proportion. Because people are fighting to serve the Lord behind the pulpit. And those who serve there don't want other people to serve in the areas they are called for. The question is, what is serving? Another word for serving is ministry. This word has been misunderstood by many folks. Because there are people out there who think that serving means opening a church when it is mentioned. However, they are far from the truth.

As a child of the Lord, you can serve God in your classroom by helping other children who have difficulty in learning.

You can visit prisoners, sick people in their homes and hospitals. Then, share the word of God and pray with them. That's serving the Lord. You just need to discover what you are good at and use it for the advancement of the kingdom of God.

If you are a political leader like a councilor, parliamentarian, etc. use your position to advocate for the wellbeing of the less privileged member of the society. In other words, go to the parliament to bring hope and solution to their daily predicament and God will elevate you.

Chapter 1
Salvation

John 3:3 Jesus answered and said unto him, Verily, verily, I say unto thee, Except a man be born again, he cannot see the kingdom of God.

The kingdom of heaven is the kingdom of principles and they bring order. Without it, disorder might set in. So, the first step towards serving the Lord is to be born again. This is the moment you are transferred from the kingdom of darkness to the kingdom of God.

It is also the period when your spirit is recreated. In other words, you put aside your old aside put on the new man. Your spirit is quickened ad become sensitive to the things of the spirit, like forgiveness, love, confidence, faith, and so on. Your relationship with God which Adam and Eve lost in the Garden of Eden is stored. Now, you can proudly say, "Jesus Christ is my father "because you have discarded the mature of the devil ad embraced the mature of God.

The moment you are born again, is the moment you are enrolled in God's army. Remember, God is still on the mission of establishing his kingdom on earth and capturing it for his glory. In other words, you can't serve God without being born again.

When you are not born again you can't fulfil your divine purpose on earth. Remember, you can't fulfil your divine assignment without being born again. It is highly impossible. For example, Jesus Christ started his ministry at the age of thirty. After he was baptized by John the Baptist and the Holy Spirit descended upon him in the form of a dove.

If you serve God without being or again you are just laboring in vain. In other words, you are using your strength to do what you are doing. You won't please the Lord because he wants you to serve him based on your relationship with him.

The moment you are born again you are now, one with Jesus Christ our Lord. Meaning that you have his mature. His being. In other words, you can't serve a master you don't know.

That's why you must be a covenant child of the Lord if you want to serve him according to his will or desire not as a way of showing off.

Chapter 2
Build your relationship with him

"As newborn babes, desire the sincere milk of the word, that ye may grow thereby:" —1 Peter 2:2

John 17:3 And this is life eternal, that they might know thee the only true God, and Jesus Christ, whom thou hast sent.

1John 2:6 He that saith he abideth in him ought himself also so to walk, even as he walked.

Once you are born again you aren't supposed to end there. Because in the kingdom of the Lord you must desire to grow in your relationship with him. Just like in the regular realm you are born as a toddler, learn to crawl, mumble, speak half words and grow from one stage to another until you are fully mature.

Similarly, your relationship with the Lord must grow and not remain a dormant.

You aren't called to warm benches in the house of the Lord but to make a difference in his kingdom. For example, you must discover what you are good at and use it for the expansion or benefit of his Kingdom. If you are a teacher, join the Sunday school and use your knowledge to train young children to walk in the ways of the Lord. If you are an accountant by profession join the finance department of the church and keep its financial records. Furthermore, if you are gifted in the area of singing you should join the praise and worship and serve the Lord there.

Lastly, if you are a good writer join the publishing department make a difference there. For example, you can edit and proofread manuscripts before publishing. At the same time, you will learn from others and polish your talents or gifts. In other words, you have something special on the inside to make people's lives better.I remember a certain evangelist in Zimbabwe, highly anointed, sadly he has gone to be with the Lord. He was living with a disability.

However, he didn't allow his condition to hinder his relationship with the Lord and serve him. He used sign languages and somebody would be beside him in the pulpit interpreting sign languages. That's somebody who motivated me the most in my Christian walk because he didn't seek self-pity like many folks like to do he fortified his relationship with the Lord and serve him diligently.

The question is, what about you? There is nothing wrong with you. If somebody living with a disability could do it, you can achieve what the Lord has created you to be before the foundations of the world. You must desire to grow and serve God with all your resources like energy, talent, time, and so forth.

Chapter 3
Allow the Holy Spirit to lead you

Zechariah 4:6 Then he answered and spake unto me, saying, This is the word of the LORD unto Zerubbabel, saying, Not by might, nor by power, but by my spirit, saith the LORD of hosts.

Galatians 5:25 If we live in the Spirit, let us also walk in the Spirit.

When you are serving in the house of God with carnality people around you will clap hands for you. But the Lord won't be aware of what you are doing. In simple words, when it comes to serving in the kingdom of God it isn't by mighty or power but by his spirit.

One day, we were working in the house of the Lord, clearing bushes to be precise. As the sun came hotter and hotter we looked for cool shades and rested. We kept the atmosphere around us alive by sharing the scriptures, engaged in the spirit of meditations and prayer.

Suddenly a humming sound grabbed our attention and the car of the church founder emerged round the corner. Guess what happened, everybody leaped to their feet and grabbed rakes, spades and started working again under the boiling sun of Africa. However, I remained under the trees and told them that what they were doing was wrong. Because they couldn't deceive the Lord. The Holy Spirit should lead us when serving the Lord. That's what is called in the fear of man, not of God.

In other words, you don't serve in the house of the Lord to please his servants. You must allow the spirit of the Lord to guide you. In the absence of a servant of the Lord, when you see chairs laying around you must take care of them. That's to say, you should stack them nicely along the walls. Remember, you can hide from a servant of the Lord but you can't hide away from God. Because he is omnipresent.

If you obey the voice of the Holy Spirit you are going to make a huge impact in this world even in the house of the Lord.

If you are led by the Holy Spirit you will win souls for the Lord without church leadership breathing on your neck. You will hit the share button on social media platforms like Facebook, Twitter, and so on and spread the gospel of Jesus Christ to the four corners of the world. If you are looking at the life of Jesus Christ he was very powerful in the spirit and in the natural realm. Because the spirit controls the physical. A man who has unlimited influence in the spirit is a destructive, machine to the kingdom of darkness. Christ's dominion on earth was tied to his obedience to the spirit of the living God. That's why he healed the sick, raise the dead and demons screamed when they came within his radius. That's a man who allowed the spirit of the Lord to guide him.

Serving God without the Holy Spirit is very destructive and won't bears any fruits. Because God and his spirit are one. If you don't have his spirit you don't have him. If you disobey the voice of the Holy Spirit you have disobeyed God. So as a covenant child of the living God you should allow the spirit of the Lord to lead you and be what the Lord has created you to be. That's to say, serving him.

Chapter 4
Put other people's needs before yours

John 13:1 Now before the feast of the passover, when Jesus knew that his hour was come that he should depart out of this world unto the Father, having loved his own which were in the world, he loved them unto the end.

John 13:2 And supper being ended, the devil having now put into the heart of Judas Iscariot, Simon's *son*, to betray him;

John 13:3 Jesus knowing that the Father had given all things into his hands, and that he was come from God, and went to God;

John 13:4 He riseth from supper, and laid aside his garments; and took a towel, and girded himself.

John 13:5 After that he poureth water into a bason, and began to wash the disciples' feet, and to wipe *them* with the towel wherewith he was girded. **John 13:6** Then cometh he to Simon Peter: and Peter saith unto him, Lord, dost thou wash my feet?

John 13:7 Jesus answered and said unto him, What I do thou knowest not now; but thou shalt know hereafter.

John 13:8 Peter saith unto him, Thou shalt never wash my feet. Jesus answered him, If I wash thee not, thou hast no part with me. **John 13:9** Simon Peter saith unto him, Lord, not my feet only, but also *my* hands and *my* head.

John 13:10 Jesus saith to him, He that is washed needeth not save to wash *his* feet, but is clean every whit: and ye are clean, but not all.

John 13:11 For he knew who should betray him; therefore said he, Ye are not all clean.

John 13:12 So after he had washed their feet, and had taken his garments, and was set down again, he said unto them, Know ye what I have done to you?

John 13:13 Ye call me Master and Lord: and ye say well; for *so* I am. **John 13:14** If I then, *your* Lord and Master, have washed your feet; ye also ought to wash one another's feet. **John 13:15** For I have given you an example, that ye should do as I have done to you.

John 13:16 Verily, verily, I say unto you, The servant is not greater than his lord; neither he that is sent greater than he that sent him.

John 13:17 If ye know these things, happy are ye if ye do them.

John 13:18 I speak not of you all: I know whom I have chosen: but that the scripture may be fulfilled, **He that eateth bread with me hath lifted up his heel against me. Matthew 14:13** When Jesus heard *of it*, he departed thence by ship into a desert place apart: and when the people had heard *thereof*, they followed him on foot out of the cities. **Matthew 14:14** And Jesus went forth, and saw a great multitude, and was moved with compassion toward them, and he healed their sick. **Matthew 14:15** And when it was evening, his disciples came to him, saying, This is a desert place, and the time is now past; send the multitude away, that they may go into the villages, and buy themselves victuals.

Matthew 14:16 But Jesus said unto them, They need not depart; give ye them to eat.

Matthew 14:17 And they say unto him, We have here but five loaves, and two fishes.

Matthew 14:18 He said, Bring them hither to me.

Matthew 14:19 And he commanded the multitude to sit down on the grass, and took the five loaves, and the two fishes, and looking up to heaven, he blessed, and brake, and gave the loaves to *his* disciples, and the disciples to the multitude.

Matthew 14:20 And they did all eat, and were filled: and they took up of the fragments that remained twelve baskets full.

Matthew 14:21 And they that had eaten were about five thousand men, beside women and children.

If you want God to empower you the more you must serve other people. That's why Jesus Christ gathered his followers and washed their feet. This shows that in the kingdom of the Lord greatness isn't about material accumulation but by serving others.

Throughout Jesus Christ's life on earth, he was serving other people not the other way round. For example, he would bless five loaves of bread and two fishes and feed the multitudes. He would go around healing the brokenhearted, setting the captive free, and so on. That's what serving is all about. If you want God to anoint you more start serving others. You shouldn't be served. For example, you must visit sick people in hospitals, prisoners, depressed, street children, and so on. Then, share the word of the Lord with them and pray with them. Don't wait for people to come to you. You should go to where problems are and be a savior there.

Putting other people's before you involve interceding for them in your secret room of prayer. In other words, when you see widows, widowers, street children, and so forth there must be a tear in your voice and not ridicule them. During Valentine's days, you should shower them with gifts like sweets because they have nobody to love them. But God who dwells in the realm of eternity loves them and he can reveal his love to them through that. That's serving.

When you are a leader and you behave like a servant doing things like participating in cleaning campaigns and so forth, that's putting other people's needs before yours. Furthermore, if you stop saying, "God bless me" and start saying "God bless so and so." You are putting other people's needs before yours and that's serving God. Because you make other people's situations your concern. In simple words, the spirit of individualism must stop, and putting other people's needs and wants before yours must emerge. That's the spirit of humility in its purest form.

Chapter 5
Don't allow situations to stop you from serving the Lord

Romans 8:35 Who shall separate us from the love of Christ? *shall* tribulation, or distress, or persecution, or famine, or nakedness, or peril, or sword?

Romans 8:36 As it is written, **For thy sake we are killed all the day long; we are accounted as sheep for the slaughter.**

In this world, one thing is certain whatever pleases the Lord attracts opposition from the kingdom of darkness. So when you are serving God you are going to be oppressed and attacked by the forces of darkness. Even people who are closer to you are going to attack you. So, as a covenant child of the living God when you are laboring for the benefits of the kingdom of God you should expect a bumpy road, not a smooth one.

When you are opposed you must deepen your love for the Lord. Because that is the only tool you can use to overcome situations and remain focused on what you are doing. You must expect your friends, family, and those who are in your community to call you all manner of names. But don't allow situations to stop you from serving in the house of the Lord .When Jesus Christ was o earth he suffered massive attacks mounted by his countrymen and women. They nearly stoned to death after calling God his father. Traditionalists were always at his throat but he loved God with all his entire beings even unto death.

Apostles like Paul and Silas were thrown into prison because those in authority wanted them to denounce their faith. However, God gave them the grace to sail through those harsh chapters. Above all, they loved serving the lord despite the challenges that erupted across their paths. Similarly, when people turn their back on you come closer to the Lord. Let your relationship with him intensify. Nothing should stop you from evangelizing, cleaning the house of the Lord, and so forth. What maintained King David in serving the Lord was his awareness that God loved him. That's why he said in Psalm 23, even though he walked through the valley of death he shall fear no evil because God was with him. As a covenant child of the living God, you should serve him with confidence knowing that he loves you.

When the devil throws darts of fear, doubts, self-pity, and so on just shot to your feet and say, "God I know you love me and I will serve you diligently. Because you are watching every step I take." If you speak like that nothing is going to stop you from serving in the kingdom of God.

Chapter 6
Love is the master key

Matt 22:36 Master, which *is* the great commandment in the law?

Matt 22:37 Jesus said unto him, **Thou shalt love the Lord thy God with all thy heart, and with all thy soul, and with all thy mind.**

Matt 22:38 This is the first and great commandment.

Matt 22:39 And the second *is* like unto it, **Thou shalt love thy neighbour as thyself.**

When you are serving in the kingdom of the Lord you must allow divine love to lead you. Remember, there are two types of love namely, natural and divine love. Natural love is influenced by what you see, feel, and so on. In other words, you are not influenced by the Holy Spirit. While divine love is influenced by the spirit of God. It is also known as agape love or God's kind of love. It is unconditional love.

If you have unconditional love you will be led by the Holy Spirit to serve the Lord and others. You will not judge other people because of the color of their skin, ethnicity, and the like. In simple words, you will view them from the perspective of God. You won't ill-treat the masses and favorably treat rich people. For example, you won't give poor people mattresses to sit on and give wealthy people luxurious and comfortable couches. You will treat everybody with the respect and love they deserve.

If you serve the lord out of unconditional love you are going to be great in his kingdom because he is looking for such. To make a positive impact in the lives of others, you won't be rude to elderly people. You will treat them with respect. No matter how much you are anointed you must treat them with utmost respect and love. S

erving God without love is a futile attempt because love is the master key to walking in the miraculous and divine wisdom. If you want to attract favours from the Lord be a bearer of his divine love.

Above all, it is the nature and the foundation of his kingdom. There is a simple rule in this world, you can't serve somebody you don't love. You must serve in the kingdom out of love not what God can give to you. If you serve the Lord because you want to be blessed I fear for you, you won't last in the service you are offering him.

Chapter 7
Test spirits

1John 4:1 Beloved, believe not every spirit, but try the spirits whether they are of God: because many false prophets are gone out into the world.

1John 4:2 Hereby know ye the Spirit of God: Every spirit that confesseth that Jesus Christ is come in the flesh is of God:

1John 4:3 And every spirit that confesseth not that Jesus Christ is come in the flesh is not of God: and this is that *spirit* of antichrist, whereof ye have heard that it should come; and even now already is it in the world.

When you are labouring for the benefit of the kingdom of God you must be able to test the spirit. Because what pleases the Lord attracts opposition from the kingdom of darkness. Don't think the devil will reveal himself to you as disfigured being with pointed horns and a forked tail.

He usually comes to children of God as an angel of light. In other words, he comes as a human being or uses a human vessel. While deep down in his heart he is planning your destruction.

Therefore, when you serve in the house of the Lord you should ask God the grace to identify the spirit of the enemy and his agents. In other words, you must be able to discern the voice of the devil and rebuke it accordingly. For example, one day Jesus Christ was revealing to his followers about his death, burial, and resurrection when Peter leaped out of nowhere and started to the speak what wasn't in line with the plan of the Lord. Guess what happened Jesus Christ rebuked him strongly because he realized the devil was using him to oppose the execution of God's plan concerning his life.

Remember, everything that shines isn't a blessing. Some of the doors are swung open by the devil to capture you. In other words, if you don't test spirits you are going to embrace the devil's manipulative lies. If you have embraced his nature you aren't going to serve the Lord in truth and spirit. You will gather brethren after service and preach what opposes what was preached during the church service. Something which is destructive and dangerous by nature.

When you are busy serving the Lord, Satan is going to send his agents in the house of the Lord to disrupt you. If you want to counterattack it you must be able to test the spirits and deal with them accordingly. Because it's not every spirit that belongs to the Lord. Satan is busy using bogus anointing to attack and deceive those who are serving the Lord in truth and spirit.

Chapter 8
Signs that a door is from the Lord

1 Corinthians 16:9 For a great door and effectual is opened unto me, and *there are* many adversaries.

Not every open door is from the Lord. Therefore as a covenant child of God, you must be in the spirit of meditation and prayer to avoid temptations. Serving in the kingdom of the Lord doesn't give you the license to step inside every door you see. Some of them are the devil's traps.

When you want to serve in the kingdom of god you must be alert because the devil is going to present his counterfeit doors before you. So, it is always advisable to detect it well in time and avoid it. For example, one day a certain brother in the Lord approached me and told me that a particular man driving a luxurious car approached him. And asked him to join their secret society and they would give him influence and wealth in return. Then, he asked him to give him enough time to think about it. Instantly, I realized it's not a Godly association and told him that it was wrong to join any group whose foundation contradicts the word of the Lord. Don't get me wrong, it isn't wrong for a covenant child of the Lord to accumulate massive wealth. But what is important is how he or she has acquired it. In simple words, it was a demonic door.

The question is how do you differentiate between satanic and Godly doors? It is quite simple, anything that is presented before you as an opportunity but isn't supported by the scriptures is not from the good Lord. Because the Lord will not contradict his word. Therefore, when God swung doors open for you it is always aligned with his word. While ungodly opportunities are always parallel to the provision of the Holy Scriptures.For example, if somebody approaches you and offers you an opportunity to work as a stripper and you are a child of the Lord, no matter how much he or she promises you don't take it. It is the devil's opportunity to entangle you into his demonic web.

Get out of that environment immediately. Many people have been offered high-paying jobs overseas only to find out they have been deceived and ended up working as prostitutes. That's to say, walking down the streets wearing revealing clothes to attract potential clients. At the end of the day being sexually, mentally, and psychologically abused. So, it is of utmost importance to ask God the grace to give you the ability to discern doors. Remember, if you leap inside every door that has been opened for you, one thing is certain you are putting your life in danger. Because isn't everything that glitters that is gold. Lastly, when demonic doors are opened for you, you won't face any resistance. Because the devil won't fight his will. So, any door that you enter with ease please, faint at the Lord's feet and repent because the enemy is about to consume your destiny. If you face opposition when you are about to enter any door, know that it is from the Lord. Because the devil fights everything that comes from God. So, if you want to serve in the kingdom of God, don't enter every door. You must cultivate a habit of asking God in prayer and he is faithful he will preserve you. Don't be in a hurry take your time and inquire from the Lord.

Chapter 9
Serve the Lord with all your heart, soul, and spirit.

1Samuel 12:24 Only fear the LORD, and serve him in truth with all your heart: for consider how great *things* he hath done for you.

Serving God shouldn't only be in words. Because words won't mobilize the Lord's vision concerning his kingdom. You must place relevant resources for it to be fulfilled on earth. Your resources could be your energy, valuable time, and everything you own.

For example, if the church of God is about to conduct a youth conference you can pledge money for their food. You can also offer them transportation, cover the cost of printing materials and so on. That's serving the Lord with everything you have.

Remember, what you have is borrowed from the Lord. Meaning the car you drive, your entire being, and the like come from the Lord who created heaven and the earth. So, you must use them for the advancement of the kingdom of the Lord on earth. During evangelism exercise, you can buy people packets of biscuits that's something. There is nothing too small in the kingdom of the Lord. If that's what you can offer, you have done your best in the eyes of the Lord.

If you don't have material things to offer in the house of the Lord you can offer your energy and quality time. For example, you can clean the church before Sunday service, sanitize people's hands, clear the bushes around the church premises, and so forth. That's still serving the Lord. You see, you have something to offer in the kingdom of the Lord.

Helping children with learning difficulties is still serving in the church of the Lord. You know, the list is endless. That's why Jesus Christ served God everywhere. That's to say, in the graveyards when he raised Lazarus from the dead, by the well when he preached to a Samaritan woman. So, don't say where I should serve the Lord. Just identify the area you are gifted in and use it for the benefit of the kingdom of the Lord.

Chapter 10
Don't turn yourself into an idol

Leviticus 26:1 Ye shall make you no idols nor graven image, neither rear you up a standing image, neither shall ye set up *any* image of stone in your land, to bow down unto it: for I *am* the LORD your God. Throughout history, men and women have stepped on the scene and claimed to be used by the Lord. They gathered groups of people and brainwashed them until they couldn't form a single thought of their own. To make matters worse, they would commit all sorts of gruesome crimes because they wanted to show their devotion to them. That's the danger of allowing people to idolize you.

When you are serving in the kingdom of God you should allow your name to diminish and allow the name of the Lord to be exalted. Don't twist scriptures because you don't want people to leave your church. God will never clap hands for that.Because they should follow God out of love not being forced or intimidated. In other words, you must use God's pulpit to glorify his name, not to serve your interest. Don't allow people to faint at your feet because that's idol worshipping. And if you are in the habit of doing that you are far from serving the Lord. You are simply, serving your desires. Something which the Lord condemns without mincing words.

Serving God means allowing him to be glorified while you are lowered to nothing. Just like John the Baptist, when people flocked around Jesus Christ. He was glad and said, it is a good thing for him to be glorified while I am lowered that's serving God according to his will. Don't create robotic beings which execute every instruction you issue. That's idol worshipping and the wrath of the Lord will locate you in no time, if you don't repent and stop what you are doing. The problem today is, people, want to be worshipped and be celebrated instead of the Lord.

They twist scriptures to destroy families and the lives of people in general. That's is wrong before God.

Chapter 11
Serve the Lord without murmuring

Philippians Phil 2:14 Do all things without murmurings and disputings:
Psalms 100:2 Serve the LORD with gladness...

When you are serving the Lord you must do that without murmuring. In other words, you must serve him with a glad heart. Because complaining hiders the power of God to operate in your life and hinder your blessings. It also hinders your creativity. So, don't complain when you serving in the house of the Lord, just allow the spirit of God to lead you in what you are doing and greatness awaits you.

However, some people serve the Lord with murmuring. That's to say, they are in the kingdom of the Lord while expecting instant rewards from him. Remember, we all serve in the Kingdom of God but he rewards his servants at his appointed time and seasons. So, just serve and he will reward you for your service.

Remember, what happened to the children of Israel after exiting Egypt and started murmuring on the way to Canaan. They said it was better in Egypt than to die in the wilderness of hunger and starvation. It didn't please the Lord. You see, murmuring and serving the Lord are two parallel things. What pleases, the Lord is when his children serve him with glad hearts.

Remember, murmuring acts as a hindrance in your heart. It hiders the spirit of the living God. So, let's go off murmuring and clean the house of God with a glad heart and you will be catapulted into stardom. The more you serve God with a glad heart is the more you attract his favors. In other words, murmuring pulls you down while serving the Lord with gladness leads to promotion. Serving the Lord without complaining isn't easy because it is human nature to complain when things don't go according to their expectations. But as children of God, you can do that with the special grace of the Lord. Remember, if the word of God says serve the Lord with a glad heart, it means it is possible. Don't start to question the integrity of the word of God because he can't ask you to do what you can't achieve. To serve In the Kingdom of God without complaining.

The end

Lightning Source UK Ltd.
Milton Keynes UK
UKHW020646040522
402481UK00009B/616

9 798210 242051